The HEART of Resilient Leadership

Mastering Emotional Intelligence to Transform Teams and Organizations

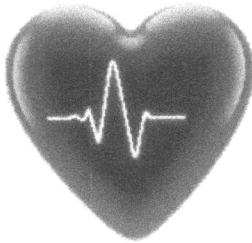

The HEART of Resilient Leadership

Dedication 5

Introduction 6

Chapter 1: 15

Defining Emotional Intelligence 15

Chapter 2: H (Harness Self-Awareness) 22

Chapter 3: E (Elevate Emotional Agility) 33

Chapter 4: A (Activate Empathy & Connection) 43

Chapter 5: R (Reinforce Purpose & Vision) 52

Chapter 6: T (Transform & Inspire Growth) 59

Chapter 7: The C.A.R.E. Approach 67

Chapter 8: Leadership Anchors 75

Chapter 9: Applying HEART Leadership to Organizational
Success 84

Chapter 10: Becoming a HEART Centered Leader: 92

A Personal Letter from Your Therapy Doctor 100

The HEART Framework 107

The C.A.R.E. Framework 108

Dedication

To Adonis, My Young Leader

You inspire me daily with your curiosity, resilience, and the kindness you show to others. May you always lead with heart, courage, and confidence. This book is dedicated to you and all future leaders as well as those who inspire us to make an impact.

Introduction

This is the *Leadership Advantage* you've been searching for!

Leadership is more demanding than ever before. The pressure to deliver results, inspire teams, and maintain your own sense of balance can feel overwhelming. It's a constant juggle between strategy, execution, and the emotional needs of your organization.

What are the emotional needs of an organization? Every thriving organization is built not only on strategy and execution, it's also built on a deep understanding of its people's emotional landscape. The emotional needs of an organization refer to the psychological and social conditions that create an environment where individuals feel valued, connected, and empowered to perform at their best. When these needs are acknowledged and nurtured, employees are more likely to engage fully, collaborate meaningfully, and lead with purpose.

In 2022, the U.S. Surgeon General released a workplace mental health framework that highlighted a growing urgency: emotional well-being is no longer a luxury, it is a necessity.

The framework identified five key conditions that support a healthy and sustainable workplace:

- Protection from harm
- Connection and community
- Work-life harmony
- A sense of value at work
- Opportunities for growth.

These are critical emotional drivers that influence morale, retention, and performance.

Organizations that intentionally address these emotional needs cultivate more than just productivity, they create cultures of trust, resilience, and innovation. When people feel emotionally safe, seen and supported, they don't just show up... they rise!

As a leader, recognizing and responding to the emotional needs of your organization is about being strategic.

You've likely experienced moments where:

- 💜 Stress clouds your decision-making, leaving you reactive instead of proactive.
- 💜 Your team seems disconnected, and you can't figure out how to bridge the gap.
- 💜 You feel isolated at the top, carrying the weight of expectations without the tools to sustain yourself emotionally.

If any of this resonates, you're not alone. The reality is, most leaders are trained to focus on metrics and outcomes, however, few are equipped with the skills to navigate the emotional dynamics that drive people, and people are what drive success. Addressing these emotional needs is imperative in leadership. Organizations that invest in psychological safety, trust, empathy, and purpose will see higher engagement, stronger retention, and greater business success. Hence, the mastering of emotional intelligence to transform teams and organizations as a healthy unit.

Here's the truth: The best leaders aren't just strategic thinkers or operational strategists. They are emotionally intelligent. The best leaders can recognize and regulate their own emotions while staying composed even under pressure. They emphasize with their teams as they create trust and engagement, build relationships, resolve conflicts and inspire action through connection. This is an incredible opportunity for leaders to master emotional intelligence and all it has to offer in terms of personal and professional benefits to living a life of harmony.

Why Emotional Intelligence is the Leadership Superpower

The concept of emotional intelligence isn't new however its application in leadership is more urgent now than ever.

Research shows that:

- 90% of top-performing leaders score high in emotional intelligence (EI).
- Teams led by emotionally intelligent leaders are more engaged, collaborative, and resilient.
- Organizations that prioritize EI in leadership report higher profitability, retention, and innovation.

The connection is clear: Emotional intelligence drives leadership effectiveness. But here's the challenge, emotional intelligence isn't something we're born with, it's a skill that requires intention, reflection, and most of all, practice.

How This Book Works

The *HEART Framework* is designed to help leaders master their emotional intelligence, create impact, and build resilient, high-performing teams.

What is the HEART framework you ask?

The *HEART framework* is a structured approach to emotionally intelligent and resilient leaders developed by "yours truly" Dr. Pauline Belton. It provides leaders with the tools to cultivate self-awareness, empathy, and adaptability, ensuring they can navigate challenging situations, inspire teams and drive sustainable success within teams and organizations.

The HEART Framework:

At the core of this book is the *HEART Framework*, a practical model for resilient, emotionally intelligent leadership:

- ♥ **Harness Self-Awareness:** Understand yourself before leading others.
- ♥ **Elevate Emotional Agility:** Learn to regulate emotions and respond to challenges with clarity.
- ♥ **Activate Empathy & Connection:** Foster strong relationships and trust.
- ♥ **Reinforce Purpose & Vision:** Align leadership with your core values and inspire your team.
- ♥ **Transform & Inspire Growth:** Develop future leaders and create a lasting impact.

Each chapter is designed to give you actionable strategies grounded in the five pillars of the *HEART framework*, helping you implement emotional intelligence into your daily leadership. You will also learn from real-world case studies from leaders I have worked with whom successfully leveraged emotional intelligence to overcome obstacles and create high impact teams (names and details were altered for confidentiality). Finally, reflection exercises to deepen your self-awareness and turn knowledge into practice with hands-on activities.

What You'll Gain from This Book

Leadership isn't just about strategy and decision making; it's about people. The most successful leaders know how to connect, inspire, and lead with emotional intelligence (EI). This book is your guide to mastering the EI skills that will elevate your leadership and transform your team's performance.

You'll learn how to:

- 💜 **Reduce Burnout:** Burnout is the result of chronic stress, emotional depletion and feeling undervalued. As a leader, your emotional wellbeing directly impacts those around you, your team's morale and productivity.
- 💜 **Strengthen:** Connections are strengthened by trust. Without it, collaboration suffers, innovation stalls and communication breaks down.
- 💜 **Navigate Challenges:** Every leader faces difficult moments; tough conversations, conflicts, crises, and high-pressure decisions without breathing room. Emotional intelligence equips you to handle these challenges with composure, empathy, and confidence.

❤ **Inspire Action:** authentic leaders don't just manage tasks, they inspire people to bring their best selves to work every day. When you lead with authenticity and purpose, you inspire your team to not just meet expectations but to exceed them.

Emotional intelligence is about understanding and harnessing emotions to become a stronger, more effective, and more compassionate leader.

It's important to know where you are, when trying to reach optimal Emotional Intelligence. Take this short quiz to assess your current stress level.

Test Your Stress

Be An Emotionally Intelligent Resilient Leader

Chapter 1:
Defining Emotional Intelligence

The ability to think strategically, hit targets, and drive innovation is important, however it's no longer enough. The most successful leaders aren't just the smartest in the room; they're the ones who can manage their emotions, connect deeply with others, and inspire teams to thrive under pressure.

This ability isn't tied to IQ, technical know-how, or years of experience. It's something different, something more powerful that goes beyond skill sets and knowledge. It's a deeper, more dynamic force that shapes how we lead, connect and inspire. It's called Emotional Intelligence (EI). It's the game-changer of leadership.

If you're reading this, chances are you already know that leadership isn't just about making decisions and managing workflows. You've likely felt the pressure of leading a team through uncertain times, resolving conflicts between colleagues and staff, or keeping morale high during moments of organizational disruption. Maybe you've experienced burnout yourself, wondering how to balance professional ambition with personal well-being.

Here's the truth: Emotional Intelligence is the missing link that can bridge the gap between performance and resilience. It's what turns managers into leaders, and leaders into visionaries.

What Is Emotional Intelligence?

At its core, Emotional Intelligence is the ability to recognize, understand, and manage your own emotions, while also recognizing, influencing, and responding to the emotions of others.

It's the difference between reacting impulsively and responding thoughtfully. It's the ability to stay calm during conflict, empathize with your team, and lead with confidence without letting stress or frustration dictate your actions.

In leadership, Emotional Intelligence shows up in three major ways:

- ♥ How you handle pressure and setbacks.
- ♥ How you build trust and relationships.
- ♥ How you influence and inspire your team.

Daniel Goleman, the psychologist and author who popularized the concept of EI, identifies *five key pillars that make up emotional intelligence:*

- ♥ **Self-Awareness:** Knowing what you feel and why you feel it.
- ♥ **Self-Regulation:** Managing your emotions and impulses, especially under stress.
- ♥ **Motivation:** Driving forward with purpose and optimism.
- ♥ **Empathy:** Understanding and considering the feelings of others.
- ♥ **Social Skills:** Navigating relationships, building networks, and resolving conflict.

These five elements don't just shape how you lead, they shape how your team perceives you, how loyal they are, and how effectively you can inspire action.

Why Emotional Intelligence Matters in Leadership

It's easy to believe that leadership is about cold, calculated decisions. Numbers, strategies, and plans drive business, right?

Well, yes, but numbers and strategies don't inspire people. People inspire people.

People are emotional beings. Whether we acknowledge it or not, emotions drive decisions, shape workplace culture, and influence performance. Leaders who understand this, who know how to regulate their own emotions and respond to the emotions of others are the ones who build high-performing, loyal teams that go the extra mile.

Your Leadership Pain Points: Addressing the Challenges

Let's get real for a second. Leadership, at its core, can be isolating.

- ♥ Have you ever felt disconnected from your team, even though you're in charge?
- ♥ Do you struggle to manage stress and stay composed in high-pressure situations?
- ♥ Is burnout creeping in, even as you try to inspire others to stay motivated?
- ♥ Are you seeing disengagement or frustration in your team, but are unsure how to address it?

These aren't just personal challenges; they're leadership warning signs. And ignoring them can lead to higher turnover, lower productivity, and ultimately, diminished influence.

Emotional Intelligence offers a transformative solution. When you master the ability to stay calm under pressure, empathize with your team, and foster collaboration, you don't just lead; you create a culture of trust, loyalty, and performance.

Emotional Intelligence (EI) vs. IQ: The Real Differentiator

You might be wondering, isn't intelligence enough? Let's break it down. IQ helps you solve problems, analyze data, and think critically, while EI helps you lead people, navigate relationships, and inspire action.

The difference?

IQ gets you in the room. Emotional Intelligence keeps you there.

Consider two technically qualified executives with equal expertise. One possesses strong emotional awareness and effectively builds relationships, motivating others. The other struggles to communicate and inspire. When adversity strikes, the first leader thrives because their team trusts and follows their lead. The second type of leader will typically experience staff discord, turnover and workplace strife.

People don't quit jobs, they quit bosses. Emotional Intelligence ensures you're the kind of boss people want to stay with, learn from, and grow alongside.

What Emotional Intelligence Looks Like in Action

Scenario 1:

A major project falls behind schedule, and the pressure mounts. A leader with low emotional intelligence reacts impulsively blaming team members, expressing frustration, and micro-managing every step. Morale drops, and the team disengages. Frustration and lack of buy-in causes the project quality to be substandard and the team to be fractured.

Scenario 2:

In the same situation, a leader with high emotional intelligence takes a different approach. They acknowledge the setback, regulate their frustration, and rally the team with empathy and focus. Instead of assigning blame, they seek solutions, empowering the team to solve problems collectively.

The predictable outcome? The emotionally intelligent leader's team feels supported, motivated, and more invested in the project's success leading to a positive outcome and cohesive team.

The Road Ahead

Mastering Emotional Intelligence isn't about perfection; it's about progress.

This book will take you on a journey, where you will experience the *HEART* of Resilient Leadership, The Wellness-Centered Feedback Formula introducing the *"C.A.R.E."* Approach, and the Three Anchors at the *HEART* of Resilient Leadership.

Let's start you down the path to emotional intelligence, let's transform the way you lead, communicate, and inspire your team.

Your leadership edge starts here.

Chapter 2: H (Harness Self-Awareness)

Why Leaders Struggle with Self-Awareness

Leadership is about understanding yourself first. As a leader, your emotions don't just influence your state of mind, they shape your decisions, impact your communication, and set the emotional tone for your entire team and the organization.

Many leaders unknowingly create tension, disengagement, and confusion within their teams because they lack self-awareness. Leaders can fall into patterns that erode trust and collaboration when self-awareness is missing.

When leaders operate without a clear understanding of their emotions, behaviors, and impact, they mistakenly foster discord and distrust. Not because they lack skills or intelligence, it's because they lack self-awareness.

Here's the truth: Developing self-awareness isn't about perfection, it's about progress. Leaders who actively cultivate self-awareness are better equipped to adapt to challenges, communicate authentically by understanding

22

their emotional tone, and model emotional intelligence by fostering trust and collaboration.

Without self-awareness, leadership can feel like navigating without a compass; reactive instead of intentional, scattered instead of strategic.

Understanding the Power of Self-Awareness

Self-awareness is the cornerstone of emotional intelligence. It is the ability to accurately perceive your own emotions and understand how they affect your thoughts, behavior, and relationships.

For leaders, self-awareness means knowing:

- ♥ What motivates you? How do you respond under pressure?
- ♥ How do your emotions impact your team?

Leaders who embody self-awareness are better equipped to:

- ♥ Adapt to challenges with clarity and composure.
- ♥ Communicate authentically by understanding their emotional tone.
- ♥ Model emotional intelligence for their teams, fostering trust and collaboration.

💙 Let's pause for a moment and take a look at a case study involving two leaders I've had the pleasure of working with, Alex and Ava.

Leaders like Alex and Ava often face challenges in self-awareness because of:

💙 **Busy schedules:** A packed calendar leaves little time for introspection.

💙 **Focus on Outcomes:** Pressure to deliver results can overshadow personal reflection.

💙 **Emotional Blind Spots:** Without feedback, it's hard to see how emotions influence leadership behavior.

However, developing self-awareness isn't about perfection, it's about progress. There's a process to develop self-awareness in order to make progress. By committing to this practice, you can elevate your leadership to new heights.

When your attention is scattered, failing to recognize how your actions influence others or how external systems shape your decisions, you risk leading without intention. Leadership without awareness can feel like walking on shaky ground, where reactions replace strategy, and clarity gives way to uncertainty. To lead effectively, you must cultivate presence, anchor yourself in self-awareness, and build the structures that keep you grounded. Only then can you create impact with confidence, authenticity, and purpose.

Identifying Emotional Triggers and Patterns That Impact Leaders

What Are Emotional Triggers?

Emotional triggers are situations, words, or behaviors that bring about a strong emotional response, often rooted in past experiences, personal values, or insecurities. These triggers can influence how you react, particularly under stress.

Why Do Emotional Patterns Matter?

As a leader, recognizing patterns in your emotional responses is essential. These patterns often dictate how you approach challenges, conflicts, and opportunities.

For example:

- 💜 Do you feel defensive when receiving feedback?
- 💜 Are you quick to anger when deadlines are missed?
- 💜 Do you avoid confrontation to maintain harmony?

By identifying these patterns, you can begin to regulate your responses, shifting from reactive to intentional leadership.

Case Study: Alex – The Reactive Leader Scenario:

Alex, a mid-level manager, prides himself on hitting deadlines and driving results. However, during a project review, a senior colleague points out a flaw in his team's work. Alex immediately feels defensive and snaps: "My team worked overtime to deliver this! Maybe you don't see the bigger picture."

Later, Alex regrets his reaction. His colleague seemed hesitant to share further insights, and his team noticed his frustration, creating tension.

Reflection: Alex realized his emotional trigger was criticism, it made him feel undervalued and insecure about his abilities. This triggered a defensive response, impacting his relationships and leadership credibility.

Practical Strategies for Alex:

1. **Pause Before Responding:** The 90-Second Rule; by taking three deep breaths before speaking during an emotionally charged moment, you create the time and space to

respond thoughtfully rather than react impulsively.

2. **Seek Context:** Instead of jumping to conclusions, ask clarifying questions when receiving feedback: "Can you elaborate on your concerns? I want to understand fully."

3. **Reflect on Triggers:** By journaling after meetings, you can identify recurring patterns and determine the root cause of the reactive behaviors. Fear of failure, physical or emotional fatigue or perhaps even financial hardships often create emotional triggers.

Case Study: Ava - The Overwhelmed Executive Scenario:

Ava, a corporate executive, is leading a team through an organizational restructure. During a meeting, a team member challenges her vision for the new structure, claiming it's unrealistic. Ava feels her heart race and struggles to suppress her frustration, dismissing the comment with a curt: "Let's move on. I've already made the decision."

Afterward, Ava notices her team seems disengaged, avoiding eye contact and hesitating to speak up. She realizes her emotional response shut down meaningful dialogue.

Reflection: Feeling threatened or undermined often causes poor emotional responses. Fear of losing authority within the team can lead to the dismissals of valid concerns.

Practical Strategies:

1. **Acknowledge Emotions in the Moment:** Practice self-awareness by internally recognizing and naming emotions during meetings (I feel frustrated and defensive), simply acknowledging these emotions can assist in regaining needed composure.

2. **Reframe the Trigger:** Instead of viewing challenges as personal attacks, reminded yourself: "Feedback is a sign of engagement and dedication. My team wants to improve this process."

3. **Follow-Up with Empathy:** Approaching team members after a meeting or engagement that may have caused tension should be focused on rebuilding trust and addressing concerns. Consider crafting a conversation with empathy,

"I realize I may have dismissed your idea earlier. Let's revisit it. I value your perspective."

Reflection Exercise:

It is important to look backward and review previous interactions reflecting on what you've learned so far:

- Identify three recent leadership situations where you experienced strong emotions.
- What emotions were present in each scenario?
- How did these emotions shape your reaction?
- If given another opportunity, how would you adjust your response?

Strategies for Strengthening Self-Awareness:

Becoming self-aware is a process that requires effort and consistency. Different strategies may appeal to different people, it is critical to explore what works for you!

Below are some strategies for consideration:

Journaling: Reflect on leadership experiences daily or weekly to assess emotional patterns and decision-making effectiveness.

Mindful Leadership Practices: Engage in mindfulness exercises, such as deep breathing or meditation, to remain present in challenging situations.

Feedback: Encourage honest feedback from peers, mentors, or direct reports to gain insights into blind spots.

Personality and EQ Assessments: Use tools like EQ-i 2.0 or DISC assessments to identify emotional intelligence strengths and areas for growth.

Key Takeaways:

- Self-awareness enhances decision-making and emotional regulation.
- Recognizing emotional triggers allows for thoughtful leadership responses.
- Developing self-awareness fosters trust, clarity, and team engagement.
- Practice Mindful Breathing: Take three deep breaths before starting any task to center your mind and reduce distractions.

"Give Yourself Permission to Lead with Resilience"
~Your Therapy Doctor ♥

Chapter 3: E (Elevate Emotional Agility)

Staying Resilient Under Pressure

The Art of Emotional Agility

In true Leadership, there is no way to avoid pressure; it's about navigating pressure with resilience and clarity. Every day, leaders face shifting priorities, unexpected challenges, and the weight of responsibility for their teams and organizations. Without emotional agility, the ability to adapt, manage emotions, and respond with intention, leaders risk burnout, decision fatigue, and fractured relationships.

Emotional agility is the secret ingredient that allows leaders to stay grounded in the face of adversity. It's not about suppressing emotions or pretending stress doesn't exist. Instead, it's about acknowledging emotions, understanding their impact, and using them as a guide rather than a roadblock. This chapter explores how leaders can cultivate emotional agility, stay composed under pressure, and lead with confidence, even in uncertain times.

What is Emotional Agility?

Emotional agility is the ability to navigate emotions effectively, rather than being controlled by them. Leaders who lack this skill often react impulsively, allowing stress, frustration, or fear to dictate their actions. On the other hand, emotionally agile leaders can pause, assess, and choose their responses with intention.

Dr. Susan David, a psychologist and researcher, describes emotional agility as having the ability to be flexible with our thoughts and emotions, so that we can respond optimally to complex situations. It's about moving through emotions, rather than being stuck in them.

Signs of Emotional Agility in Leadership:

- ♥ You acknowledge your emotions.
- ♥ You adapt quickly to setbacks.
- ♥ You regulate stress effectively.
- ♥ You communicate with clarity.
- ♥ You foster a culture of psychological safety.

The Leadership Conundrum: Why Emotional Agility Matters

Leadership can feel like a no-win situation too often.

The pressures are real:

- ♥ **High-Stakes Decision Making:** The need to make quick, informed choices that impact teams and business outcomes.
- ♥ **Emotional Labor:** Managing not only your own emotions but also the emotions of those you lead.
- ♥ **Crisis Management:** Navigating unpredictable challenges, from organizational changes to economic downturns.
- ♥ **Personal Well-Being:** Balancing work responsibilities with personal life and mental health.

Emotional agility allows you to manage pressures that could lead to burnout, disengagement, and reactive leadership. With the right tools, you can shift from being overwhelmed by pressure to mastering it.

Strategies to Build Emotional Agility

Create Space Between Emotion and Action

When an emotional reaction is triggered, your brain releases chemicals that last about 90 seconds. Instead of reacting immediately, take a deep breath through your nose with your mouth closed (counting to 7) hold for a count of 6 then exhale through your mouth (counting to 7)

In that space, ask yourself:

- 💜 What is this emotion telling me?
- 💜 What is the most productive way to respond with healthy intentions?

Example: If confronted with unexpected criticism, pause, take a breath, and respond with intention to understand rather than defensiveness. This brief pause allows you to regain control and respond intentionally rather than emotionally.

Reframe Challenges as Opportunities

The mindset with which you approach challenges shapes your ability to navigate them. A growth mindset allows you to see things from a win-win standpoint. Emotionally agile leaders embrace cognitive reframing by shifting their perspective to see obstacles as growth opportunities rather than setbacks.

Reframing in Action:

Instead of "This situation is overwhelming," try "This is an opportunity to practice resilience and adaptability."

36

Instead of "I failed," try "This experience is teaching me something valuable."

Example: If a project falls behind schedule, instead of placing blame, ask: What can we learn from this? How can we improve for the future? Reframing allows you to stay solution-focused, even in the toughest moments.

Regulate Stress Before It Regulates You

Emotional agility doesn't eliminate stress; it gives you the professional posture to manage stress effectively. Without regulation, stress can manifest as irritability, poor decision-making, or even physical symptoms like headaches and fatigue.

Quick Stress Management Techniques:

- ♥ **Box Breathing:** Inhale for four counts, hold for four, exhale for four, hold for four. Repeat for 3 minutes.
- ♥ **Body Scan Check-In:** Pause and notice where you're holding tension. Relax your shoulders, unclench your jaw, and release tension with each exhale.
- ♥ **Movement Reset:** Stand up, stretch, or take a short walk to reset your nervous system.

Making stress management a daily practice helps prevent emotional buildup. Stress management gives you the ability to face unpredictable moments of crisis with Emotional Agility.

Name Your Emotions to Manage Them

Many leaders push through stress, anger, or frustration without acknowledging what they're feeling. Research shows that simply naming emotions reduces their intensity and helps the brain process them more effectively.

When you feel overwhelmed, take a moment to label the emotion: "I feel anxious", "I feel uncertain", "I feel frustrated". Once you have named the emotion, emotions become less overpowering, allowing you to approach situations with greater clarity, calm and resilience.

Lead with Psychological Safety

Emotionally agile leaders create environments where people feel safe to express concerns, make mistakes, share ideas and feel supported. Psychological safety fosters innovation, trust, and engagement. Micromanagement creates an environment of emotional distress.

How to Build Psychological Safety

- 💜 Model vulnerability by acknowledging challenges and mistakes.
- 💜 Encourage open dialogue, ask for feedback and listen actively.
- 💜 Validate emotions rather than dismissing them. Instead of "You shouldn't feel that way", try "I understand why this is frustrating".

Case Study: Emotional Agility in Action Meet Marcus: The Leader Who Mastered Emotional Agility

Marcus, a senior executive, faced a sudden organizational restructure that left his team feeling uncertain and anxious. Initially, he felt overwhelmed himself, his mind raced with worst-case scenarios, and he noticed tension rising in his body.

Instead of reacting impulsively, Marcus applied emotional agility strategies:

- 💜 He paused before responding to his team's concerns, giving himself time to process his own emotions first.

- ♥ He reframed the challenge, seeing the restructuring as an opportunity to build a stronger, more adaptable team.
- ♥ He acknowledged emotions openly, telling his team, "I understand that change can be unsettling.

"Let's work through this together".

- ♥ He focused on what he could control, maintaining transparency, open communication, and a solution-driven mindset.

As a result, Marcus managed the transition smoothly as well as strengthened his team's trust in his leadership.

Key Takeaways

- 💜 Emotional agility is the ability to adapt, regulate emotions, and respond with intention.
- 💜 Leaders who cultivate emotional agility stay resilient under pressure and make better decisions.
- 💜 Practicing pausing before reacting, reframing challenges, regulating stress, and fostering psychological safety enhances leadership effectiveness.
- 💜 The best leaders don't avoid emotions; they navigate them with skill and purpose.

Final Reflection

Emotional agility is a lifelong practice. Each day presents a new opportunity to pause, reframe, and respond with greater wisdom. As you move forward, ask yourself: How can I use emotional agility to elevate my leadership today. True leadership is about knowing how to bend without breaking.

"Emotional intelligence transforms leadership from a position of authority to a movement of impact."

~Your Therapy Doctor 🖤

Chapter 4: A (Activate Empathy & Connection)

Leading with Human-Centered Intelligence

Empathy & Connection

As we explored in the previous chapter, emotional agility equips leaders with the ability to navigate challenges with resilience and composure. However, leadership isn't just about self-regulation; it's also about fostering meaningful connections with others. The ability to understand, support, and inspire those around you is what transforms a leader from being effective to being truly impactful.

Empathy and connection serve as the foundation of leadership that prioritizes people over processes, trust over transactions, and collaboration over command. This chapter will guide you through the essential elements of human-centered leadership—how to cultivate empathy, strengthen relationships, and create an environment where people feel valued and motivated to contribute their best work.

The Power of Connection in Leadership

Leadership is more than strategy and execution; leadership is about people. The most effective leaders cultivate trust, inspire action, and foster an environment where people feel valued and heard. At the heart of this ability lies empathy, the bridge that transforms leadership from transactional to transformational.

Empathy isn't just about understanding others; it's about actively engaging with their emotions, challenges, and perspectives. Empathy is what separates a boss from a leader and turns a workplace into a thriving community.

This chapter will explore how you can strengthen your ability to lead with empathy, build authentic connections, and create a psychologically safe environment for your team to thrive.

Why is Empathy Important in Leadership?

We've all encountered leaders who are brilliant strategists and yet they struggle to connect with their teams. Their presence commands authority, yet their leadership lacks warmth. On the surface, things seem fine however under the surface; disengagement, burnout, and quiet quitting begin to take root. Emotionally intelligent leaders recognize that people don't just work for paychecks, they work for purpose, belonging, and respect. When leaders prioritize connection, they unlock creativity, collaboration, and a deeper sense of commitment within their teams.

What Empathy in Leadership Looks Like:

- ♥ Actively listening to understand.
- ♥ Recognizing when someone is struggling and offering support appropriate for the situation.
- ♥ Being present in conversations.
- ♥ Encouraging open dialogue.
- ♥ Leading with emotional awareness.
- ♥ Asking clarifying questions to fully understand the challenge.

The Three Levels of Empathy in Leadership

Dr. Daniel Goleman, one of the leading voices in emotional intelligence, identifies three types of empathy that leaders can cultivate:

- ♥ *Cognitive Empathy* Understanding what someone else is thinking. This helps leaders anticipate concerns and perspectives before making decisions.

- 💜 **Emotional Empathy** Feeling what someone else feels. This allows leaders to build deeper trust and connections with their teams.
- 💜 **Compassionate Empathy** Taking action to support others. This is empathy in motion, when leaders go beyond understanding and feeling and actively work to improve the situation.

Resilient leaders engage in all three forms of empathy, ensuring their teams feel valued as human beings

Building a Culture of Connection

Empathy requires intention. To cultivate a culture of connection, leaders must consistently model vulnerability, authenticity, and active listening.

Master the Art of Active Listening

Most people listen to respond, not to understand. Leaders who practice active listening create space for open communication and trust.

Try This:

- 💜 Maintain eye contact and nod to show engagement.
- 💜 Use open-ended questions like, "Can you tell me more about that?"

- 💜 Summarize what was said to ensure clarity: "What I hear you saying is…"

Show Up with Authenticity

People respect leaders who are authentic and real, not perfect. When leaders express vulnerability, admitting mistakes, sharing challenges, and demonstrating self-awareness, they create an environment where others feel safe to do the same.

Try This:

- 💜 Instead of saying, "I have all the answers," try "Let's figure this out together."
- 💜 When facing challenges, share lessons learned instead of masking struggles.

Recognize and Validate Emotions

Most people want to feel seen, heard and understood especially during moments of tension, uncertainty, or excitement. When leaders take time to recognize and validate the emotions of others, they build bridges of trust, deepen relationships, and create psychologically safe spaces where people feel valued; not just for what they do but for who they are.

A simple "I see how that could be frustrating" or "That sounds really exciting, tell me more" goes a long way in making people feel heard and valued.

Try This:

- ♥ Acknowledge emotions before jumping into solutions.
- ♥ Validate concerns instead of dismissing them.

Lead with Psychological Safety

A workplace where people fear judgment or retaliation stifles innovation and collaboration. Psychological safety means fostering an environment where team members feel safe to speak up, share ideas, and even make mistakes without fear.

Try This:

- ♥ Encourage feedback by asking, "What's one thing I could do better as a leader?"
- ♥ Reward learning from mistakes instead of punishing failure.
- ♥ Normalize difficult conversations by making them routine rather than reactive.

Case Study: The Leader Who Transformed Culture Through Empathy

Meet Sophia, a senior executive at a fast-growing company. Despite her strong business acumen, she noticed her team was disengaged, hesitant to share ideas, and reluctant to take initiative. After a series of exits from key employees, she realized something had to change.

Instead of focusing solely on performance metrics, Sophia decided to prioritize connection and trust. She committed to weekly one-on-one check-ins, where she asked open-ended questions like, "How are you feeling about your workload?" and "What's one thing I can do to support you better?"

At first, the conversations were brief, over time, her team started opening up. They shared frustrations, insights, and even new ideas. Within six months, Sophia's team was more engaged as well as more innovative. Employees reported higher job satisfaction, increased motivation, and stronger collaboration.

Her secret? Leading with empathy first.

Key Takeaways

- 💜 Empathy is the foundation of trust, connection, and team engagement.
- 💜 Leading with human-centered intelligence fosters psychological safety and innovation.
- 💜 Active listening, authenticity, and emotional validation create a workplace where people feel valued.
- 💜 A culture of connection doesn't happen by accident:
- 💜 It happens by design.

Final Reflection

Take a moment to reflect: How do you show up as an empathetic leader? What's one small shift you can make today to strengthen your connection with your team?

Remember, leadership isn't about knowing it all; it's about caring enough to understand, listen, and lead with heart.

"Your ability to lead others starts with your ability to lead yourself; know your triggers, manage your emotions, and choose your impact wisely."

~Your Therapy Doctor 🖤

Chapter 5: R (Reinforce Purpose & Vision)

Aligning Leadership with Impact

As we explored in the previous chapter, empathy and connection build trust and psychological safety within a team. Empathy alone isn't enough; leaders must also have a strong sense of purpose and vision. Clarity of direction is another key component to maintain a connected, resilient team. This chapter will guide you in aligning your leadership with purpose, articulating a compelling vision, and inspiring those around you to move forward with confidence and meaning.

The Power of Purpose in Leadership

Great leaders don't just set goals; they ignite purpose. Purpose-driven leadership ensures that every decision, action, and strategy is rooted in something bigger than short-term outcomes. It fuels motivation, resilience, and commitment, qualities essential for long-term success.

Purpose-Driven Leaders:

- ❤ Inspire action by connecting daily work to a larger mission.
- ❤ Maintain focus and motivation, even in unpredictable times.
- ❤ Help their teams see the "why" behind the work, increasing engagement and ownership.
- ❤ Foster resilience, turning obstacles into opportunities for growth.

When leaders operate with purpose, they don't just direct—they empower. They cultivate an environment where individuals and teams align their efforts with shared values and long-term aspirations.

Clarifying Your Leadership Vision

A vision is more than a statement; it's a guide, a purpose and lens of focus. It gives you and your team clarity about where they're headed and why their contributions matter. Leaders with a clear vision inspire confidence, encourage innovation, and provide stability even in uncertain times.

How to Define Your Vision:

1. ***Identify Core Values*** What principles drive you as a leader? Your vision should reflect the values that shape your decisions.
2. ***Picture the Future*** Imagine your ideal team, organization, or impact five years from now. What does success look like?
3. ***Make It Tangible*** A compelling vision is clear, actionable, and easy to communicate with.
4. ***Align with Team Aspirations*** A great vision isn't created in isolation; engage your team in shaping a collective purpose. A well-defined vision gives your leadership momentum and ensures that everyone is working toward a common goal.

Communicating Purpose and Vision with Impact

A leader's purpose and vision mean little if they aren't communicated effectively. How you articulate and reinforce these ideas determines whether they become empty words or a true driving force within your organization.

1. ***Tell a Compelling Story*** People connect with stories, not just facts. When sharing your vision, use real examples, personal experiences, or team success stories to illustrate why it matters.

2. ***Reinforce the "Why" Daily*** Purpose and vision aren't one-time conversations. Regularly tie work back to the bigger mission through team meetings, one-on-ones, and recognition moments.

3. ***Lead by Example*** If your team doesn't see you embodying the vision, they won't buy in. Demonstrate commitment through your decisions, actions, and leadership style.

Empowering Others to Own the Vision

Purpose becomes more powerful when everyone feels connected to it. Involve your team in shaping initiatives, setting goals, and defining how they contribute to the broader mission.

Case Study: Transforming Leadership Through Purpose

Meet Daniel: A Leader Who Turned Vision into Impact

Daniel, a department head in a growing organization, noticed disengagement creeping into his team. Despite the clear (key performance indicators) KPIs, employees seemed uninspired and disconnected. Realizing the missing piece was purpose, Daniel took action.

1.   **He redefined the team's mission** Instead of focusing solely on hitting targets, he framed their work as a critical part of the company's broader impact on the community.

2.   **He communicated this vision daily** In meetings, he reinforced how their efforts contributed to meaningful change.

3.   **He empowered employees to shape the vision** By involving them in decision-making, they felt ownership over their contributions. The result? Engagement and motivation skyrocketed. Employees weren't just completing tasks they were invested in a shared mission.

Key Takeaways

- 💜 Purpose fuels leadership: it provides direction, motivation, and meaning.
- 💜 A compelling vision brings clarity; it aligns teams toward a shared goal.
- 💜 Effective communication transforms purpose into action; leaders must reinforce the "why" consistently.
- 💜 Empowerment creates ownership; when employees feel connected to the vision, they engage more deeply.

Final Reflection

Take a moment to ask yourself: Is my leadership rooted in purpose? How clearly have I communicated my vision to my team? What steps can I take to reinforce alignment between daily work and long-term impact? Leading with purpose is about inspiring those around you to walk that path with intention and belief.

Great leaders don't just manage people they empower them to discover their own strength."

~Your Therapy Doctor 🖤

Chapter 6: T (Transform & Inspire Growth)

Creating a Culture of Continuous Leadership Development

From Vision to Growth: A Leader's Next Step

In the previous chapter, we explored how aligning leadership with purpose and vision provides the foundation for a motivated and engaged team. But a vision alone isn't enough, it must be nurtured, adapted, and continuously reinforced through development and transformation. Leadership is not a static position; it's an evolving process that requires growth, both within yourself and in those you lead. This chapter focuses on fostering a culture of learning, adaptability, and mentorship to ensure leadership excellence is sustained across teams and generations.

Why Growth-Focused Leadership Matters

Great leaders cultivate future leaders. A growth-oriented leadership culture ensures that organizations thrive in the present and are prepared for the future. By focusing on continuous development, leaders inspire innovation, adaptability, and long-term success.

Leaders Who Prioritize Growth:

- ♥ Encourage lifelong learning and professional development.
- ♥ Adapt to change with resilience.
- ♥ Mentor and empower their teams to take ownership.
- ♥ Recognize that leadership development benefits both individuals and the organization as a whole.

When leaders invest in personal and team growth, they create an environment where people feel challenged, valued, and inspired to reach their full potential.

Fostering a Culture of Continuous Leadership Development

Leadership development requires intention, structure, and a mindset that prioritizes learning as an ongoing process.

1. **Model a Growth Mindset** Leaders set the tone. If they demonstrate a willingness to learn, seek feedback, and adapt to change, their teams will follow suit.

Try This:

- 💜 Embrace challenges as opportunities for growth.
- 💜 Be open about your own learning journey and areas for improvement.
- 💜 Encourage constructive feedback and act on it.

2. **Provide Opportunities for Learning and Development** Investing in professional growth shows your team that you value their potential. This can take the form of mentorship, training programs, or experiential learning.

Try This:

- 💜 Offer leadership development workshops or coaching sessions. (You can begin this journey by visiting www.yourtherapydoctor.com for leadership development workshops, leadership training programs, EQ-1 2.0/360 Feedback for leadership, growth and consultation).
- 💜 Encourage cross-training to expand skills beyond job descriptions.
- 💜 Support continuing education and certification opportunities.

3. **Empower Others to Lead** Leadership isn't just for those with a title. When you empower others to take on leadership roles, you cultivate a culture of shared responsibility and confidence.

Try This:

- ♥ Delegate meaningful responsibilities that challenge and grow team members.
- ♥ Recognize and celebrate leadership qualities in those around you.
- ♥ Encourage initiative and decision-making at all levels.

4. **Create Safe Spaces for Innovation and Experimentation** A growth culture thrives on innovation. Leaders who provide a safe space for new ideas and experimentation encourage creativity and problem-solving.

Try This:

- ♥ Foster brainstorming sessions where all voices are heard.
- ♥ Frame mistakes as learning experiences rather than failures.
- ♥ Encourage calculated risk-taking with support and guidance.

Case Study: Transforming a School Through Growth-Centered Leadership

Meet Principal Jackson: A Leader Who Invested in Future Leadership

When Principal Jackson took over at Maplewood Public School, he inherited a struggling environment. Teacher morale was low, student engagement was declining, and administrative turnover had become a constant challenge. Rather than focusing solely on immediate fixes, he recognized that sustainable change required a growth mindset and leadership development at all levels.

1. **He empowered teachers as leaders** Instead of making all decisions himself, he created teacher-led committees to give staff ownership over school initiatives.
2. **He invested in professional development** He allocated funding for training in leadership skills, emotional intelligence, and conflict resolution.
3. **He encouraged mentorship** Veteran teachers were paired with new educators, fostering a culture of shared learning and guidance.
4. **He embraced student leadership** Student-led programs, such as peer mentoring and leadership

councils, were introduced to encourage responsibility and involvement.

Within three years, Maplewood saw a 25% increase in teacher retention, a significant improvement in student academic engagement, and a stronger, more collaborative school culture. By prioritizing growth-centered leadership, Principal Jackson didn't just transform the school he inspired a new generation of leaders within it.

Key Takeaways

- 💜 Leadership is an evolving journey; growth must be intentional and continuous.
- 💜 A learning culture empowers teams when development is prioritized, engagement and motivation increase.
- 💜 Mentorship and shared leadership create sustainability strong teams emerge when leadership is cultivated at all levels.
- 💜 Encouraging innovation leads to resilience adaptability, which is key to navigating the ever-changing leadership landscape.

Final Reflection

Take a moment to reflect, how do I actively foster growth in myself and my team? What small step can I take today to encourage learning, leadership, or mentorship within my organization?

True leadership is not about reaching a destination, it's about continuously evolving, inspiring, and paving the way for future leaders to rise.

"Every challenge is a test of emotional agility face it with clarity, respond with intention, and grow with resilience."

~Your Therapy Doctor 🖤

Chapter 7: The C.A.R.E. Approach

The Wellness-Centered Feedback Formula

From Growth to Communication: Strengthening Leadership Through Connection

In the previous chapter, we explored the power of continuous leadership development and fostering a culture of growth. But even the best leadership strategies can fall short without one crucial element: effective communication. Leadership is not just about making decisions; it's about ensuring those decisions are understood, embraced, and executed with clarity and purpose. Communication, when infused with emotional intelligence, becomes the bridge between vision and action, between leaders and teams.

This chapter introduces the *C.A.R.E.* Approach, a framework designed to help leaders deliver feedback with empathy, clarity, and impact. By mastering communication rooted in emotional intelligence, leaders can inspire trust, reduce conflict, and create meaningful engagement with those they lead.

The C.A.R.E. Approach:

A Wellness-Centered Feedback Formula which provides a structured yet emotionally intelligent way to deliver feedback. It stands for:

- ♥ **Context:** Frame the discussion in terms of shared goals and mutual outcomes.
- ♥ **Affirmation:** Recognize strengths and contributions before addressing areas of improvement.
- ♥ **Reflection:** Invite self-awareness and collaboration instead of imposing criticism.
- ♥ **Encouragement:** End with actionable support and motivation for continued growth.

By integrating these principles, leaders can transform the way they communicate, making every interaction purposeful and impactful.

Breaking Down the C.A.R.E. Approach

Context: Setting the Stage for Constructive Dialogue

Effective feedback begins with context. Rather than diving into criticism, frame the conversation around shared goals and positive intent.

Try This:

- ♥ Start with why the discussion is important: "I want to discuss how we can streamline our teamwork to achieve our project goals more effectively."
- ♥ Avoid personal blame focus on objectives and improvements to lead with process, protocols and/or procedures instead of the person.

Affirmation: Recognizing Strengths First

People receive feedback more openly when they feel valued. Acknowledge what's working before introducing areas of growth.

Try This:

- ♥ Express appreciation for contributions: "Your dedication to meeting tight deadlines has been impressive and greatly contributes to the team's success."
- ♥ Be specific about strengths, making the affirmation feel genuine.

Reflection: Inviting Growth Through Self-Awareness

Encourage individuals to reflect on their performance rather than imposing judgments. This fosters engagement and accountability.

Try This:

💜 Use open-ended questions: "I noticed there have been challenges with time management recently. Can you share your perspective on this?" • Keep the tone supportive, not confrontational.

Encouragement: Ending with Support and Motivation

Feedback should leave individuals feeling empowered, not discouraged. Offer guidance, resources, or a collaborative approach to improvement.

Try This:

💜 Express confidence in their ability to grow: "I'm confident that with a clearer structure, you can overcome this hurdle. Let's work together to identify tools or strategies that might help."

💜 Reinforce their potential and provide actionable next steps.

Why the C.A.R.E. Approach Stands Out

- 💜 **Mental Health Support:** Encourages a nonjudgmental and collaborative tone, reducing stress and promoting a sense of safety.
- 💜 **Empathy-Driven:** Focuses on understanding the individual's perspective before addressing concerns.
- 💜 **Encouragement as the Core:** Ends with positivity and actionable solutions, fostering motivation and resilience.
- 💜 **Scalable for Leaders:** Applies universally across teams and organizational levels, emphasizing emotional intelligence.

Case Study: A Director of Nursing Who Led with C.A.R.E.
Meet Director Patel: Transforming Feedback into Growth
Medical Director Patel faced significant challenges in her department; her team felt overworked, underappreciated, and disconnected from leadership. This led to high-stress levels, reduced morale, and increased turnover. Instead of enforcing strict policies or micromanaging staff, she chose to shift her approach to feedback using the *C.A.R.E.* Approach.

- ♥ **Context:** She started every feedback session by framing discussions around shared patient care goals and team well-being.
- ♥ **Affirmation:** She made it a point to recognize the dedication and long hours her nurses put in before addressing any areas for improvement.
- ♥ **Reflection:** She invited nurses to share their perspectives on workload challenges, fostering open dialogue and collaboration.
- ♥ **Encouragement:** She implemented support programs, wellness initiatives, and professional development opportunities to help nurses feel empowered and valued.

Within a year, nurse retention improved by 35%, workplace stress decreased, and staff reported feeling more engaged and appreciated. By prioritizing emotionally intelligent communication, Director Patel transformed her department's culture and strengthened leadership at all levels.

Key Takeaways

- 🖤 Context frames feedback positively ensuring alignment with shared goals.
- 🖤 Affirmation builds trust helping individuals feel valued before discussing improvements.
- 🖤 Reflection fosters accountability shifting from directive to collaborative conversations.
- 🖤 Encouragement fuels growth providing motivation and resources for success.

Final Reflection

Think about your recent feedback conversations. Were they constructive, supportive, and empathetic? How can you apply the *C.A.R.E.* Approach in your daily interactions to build stronger relationships and foster growth?

Feedback isn't about pointing out faults, it's about empowering people to reach their full potential. Leading with *C.A.R.E.* ensures that every conversation is an opportunity for connection, confidence, and continuous improvement.

"When you master emotional intelligence, leadership becomes less about power and more about purpose."

~Your Therapy Doctor 💜

Chapter 8: Leadership Anchors

The Pillars of Transformational Leadership

The Foundation of Lasting Leadership

In the previous chapter, we explored the power of effective communication and emotional intelligence in leadership.

But strong communication alone is not enough. To truly transform teams and organizations, leaders must anchor themselves in principles that provide stability, direction, and inspiration. Leadership is a continuous journey requiring depth, connection, and intentionality.

Transformational leadership is built on three essential anchors: a structured process, strong relationships, and the ability to inspire. These anchors create the foundation for leadership that goes beyond task management and fosters genuine impact. When leaders embrace these principles, they elevate, empower, and create lasting change.

Leadership as a Process: The Path to Clarity and Direction

A leader without a process is like a ship without a compass. Processes provide structure and intentionality, ensuring that actions align with goals. They create a framework for decision-making, problem-solving, and growth—not just for the leader but for the entire team.

The Components of a Transformational Process:

- ♥ **Vision and Strategy:** Clear objectives that align with organizational values and long-term goals.
- ♥ **Adaptability:** The flexibility to refine the process as challenges and opportunities arise.
- ♥ **Consistency:** A reliable approach that builds trust and predictability within the team.

Example in Practice: A transformational leader uses a structured process like the *HEART Framework* (Harness, Elevate, Activate, Reinforce, Transform) to foster emotional intelligence and growth within their team. By harnessing self-awareness, elevating emotional agility, activating empathy, reinforcing purpose, and transforming leadership, leaders create ripple effects of positive change.

Processes give leaders clarity, but they also empower teams by setting clear expectations and providing tools to succeed. With the right process in place, leadership becomes a steady, intentional journey rather than a series of reactive decisions.

Leadership as a Relational Concept: The Heart of Connection with C.A.R.E.

Leadership thrives in relationships. Transformational leaders understand that connection not control is the key to influence. By fostering trust, empathy, and communication, leaders build relational equity that enables them to inspire and empower others.

The Pillars of Relational Leadership:

- 💜 **Empathy:** Understanding and validating the emotions and perspectives of others.
- 💜 **Authenticity:** Leading with honesty, vulnerability, and integrity.
- 💜 **Communication:** Actively listening and delivering clear, transparent messages.

Using the C.A.R.E. Approach for Stronger Leadership Relationships:

- ❤ **Context:** Establish a clear purpose for discussions and ensure alignment with team goals.
- ❤ **Affirmation:** Recognize individual contributions before addressing challenges.
- ❤ **Reflection:** Encourage open dialogue and invite team members to share insights.
- ❤ **Encouragement:** Offer constructive feedback with a focus on growth and support.

Relational Leadership in Action

Consider a leader who prioritizes one-on-one conversations with team members, ensuring that each individual feels heard, valued, and supported. This leader recognizes that relationships are not transactional but foundational to building a cohesive, motivated team.

By focusing on relationships and applying the *C.A.R.E.* Approach, leaders create a culture of psychological safety, where team members feel confident to share ideas, take risks, and innovate. This relational approach fosters loyalty, collaboration, and mutual respect.

The Ability to Inspire: Leadership's Transformative Power

Inspiration is the spark that turns vision into reality. While processes provide structure and relationships foster trust, inspiration ignites action and drives engagement. Transformational leaders inspire by connecting deeply with their teams and instilling a shared sense of purpose.

How Leaders Inspire:

- ♥ **Visionary Thinking:** Painting a compelling picture of the future that motivates others to strive for excellence.
- ♥ **Leading by Example:** Demonstrating the values, resilience, and work ethic they wish to see in their teams.
- ♥ **Encouragement:** Recognizing and celebrating progress to keep morale and motivation high.

Example of Inspirational Leadership: Think of a leader who rallies their team during a challenging time by sharing a personal story of resilience and growth. Their vulnerability and vision remind the team of their shared purpose, sparking renewed commitment and energy.

Inspiration transforms leadership from transactional to transformational. It's the force that makes people not only follow but also believe in the journey.

Case Study: A Supervising Engineer Who Led with Anchors Meet Engineer Thompson: Strengthening Leadership Through Process, Connection, and Inspiration As a supervising engineer overseeing a team of project managers, Thompson encountered significant challenges; tight deadlines, conflicting priorities, and team members feeling disconnected from leadership. Instead of enforcing rigid policies or micromanaging, he chose to anchor his leadership in process, relationships, and inspiration.

Process: Thompson implemented the *HEART* model to create a structured yet flexible workflow, ensuring efficiency while allowing adaptability.

Relationships: He applied the *C.A.R.E.* Approach, holding regular check-ins to provide feedback, recognize achievements, and encourage open dialogue.

Inspiration: Recognizing the pressure of engineering work, he frequently highlighted team successes, shared industry innovations, and reminded his team of their critical role in shaping the future.

Within a year, team productivity improved, communication strengthened, and morale increased. By integrating process, relational leadership, and inspiration, Engineer Thompson cultivated a thriving, motivated team that consistently delivered excellence.

Bringing It All Together: The Three Anchors in Harmony
When leadership is anchored in process, relationships, and inspiration, it transcends the ordinary. These three elements work together to create a synergy that empowers teams, fosters innovation, and drives lasting success. Leaders who embrace these anchors; transform individuals, teams, and organizations.

Great leadership starts with intentionality. By focusing on these three anchors, you can elevate your leadership from good to transformational, creating impact that resonates far beyond the workplace.

Final Reflection

- ♥ Take a moment to assess your leadership approach:
- ♥ Are your decisions guided by a clear and adaptable process?
- ♥ Are you building meaningful relationships that foster trust and collaboration?
- ♥ Are you inspiring others to believe in their potential and shared purpose?

Transformation happens when leadership is anchored in stability, connection, and vision. By reinforcing these three pillars, you ensure that your leadership legacy is about the people and culture you elevate along the way.

"A leader's greatest strength isn't in knowing all the answers, it's creating space for others to grow alongside them."

~Your Therapy Doctor

Chapter 9: Applying HEART Leadership to Organizational Success

Translating Leadership into Organizational Impact

In the previous chapters, we explored the foundational elements of transformational leadership, from structured processes to relational leadership and the power of inspiration. Now, it's time to take these principles and apply them at an organizational level. Leadership isn't just about individual effectiveness, it's about creating cultures of trust, innovation, and resilience that drive long-term success.

The *HEART Framework* (Harness, Elevate, Activate, Reinforce, Transform) provides a roadmap for embedding emotional intelligence into leadership, ensuring that organizations are not only productive but also people centered. Leaders who apply *HEART* principles create environments where employees feel valued, teams collaborate seamlessly, and performance aligns with purpose.

Embedding the HEART Framework into Organizational Success

1.   **Harness Self-Awareness:**
  - ♥ Leaders set the tone for the entire organization. Self-awareness ensures leaders manage their emotions effectively and model emotional intelligence for their teams.
  - ♥ Organizations can cultivate this by offering executive coaching, leadership reflection exercises, and emotional intelligence assessments.

2.   **Elevate Emotional Agility:**
  - ♥ Change is inevitable, but emotionally agile organizations adapt with resilience. Leaders must encourage flexibility, promote psychological safety, and model calm decision-making under pressure.
  - ♥ Implementing wellness programs, open communication channels, and stress management strategies supports emotional agility at every level.

3. *Activate Empathy & Connection:*

💜 Strong relationships fuel strong organizations. Leaders must foster empathy in decision-making, ensuring that employees, customers, and stakeholders feel understood and valued.

💜 Regular feedback sessions, mentorship programs, and initiatives strengthen organizational empathy.

4. *Reinforce Purpose & Vision:*

💜 A shared mission unites teams and motivates performance. Leaders should consistently communicate vision and ensure that every team member sees their role in the bigger picture.

💜 Aligning company values with daily operations, reinforcing vision in team meetings, and recognizing employees' contributions builds alignment and engagement.

5. *Transform & Inspire Growth:*

💜 Transformational leadership is about developing others. Organizations thrive when they prioritize leadership development, encourage innovation, and celebrate continuous learning.

💜 Investment in leadership training, career development paths, and mentorship cultivates an organizational culture of growth and excellence.

Case Study: A Chief of Police Who Led with HEART

Meet Chief Daniels: Transforming a Police Department Through HEART Leadership

Chief Daniels took over a police department struggling with internal conflict, low morale, and declining community trust. Recognizing that enforcement alone wouldn't create sustainable change, he decided to implement the *HEART* leadership model to rebuild relationships, trust, and organizational excellence.

1. **Harnessing Self-Awareness:** Daniels started by assessing his own leadership approach, seeking feedback from officers, city officials, and community leaders to understand his blind spots and areas for improvement.

2. **Elevating Emotional Agility:** He introduced emotional intelligence training for officers, helping them manage stress, navigate high-pressure situations, and communicate effectively with both colleagues and the public.

3. **Activating Empathy & Connection:** To bridge the gap between law enforcement and the

community, Daniels prioritized community outreach initiatives, increased transparency in department decisions, and encouraged officers to participate in local events.

4. **Reinforcing Purpose & Vision:** He redefined the department's mission, emphasizing service, integrity, and accountability. Regular briefings reinforced this vision, connecting officers to a greater purpose beyond law enforcement.

5. **Transforming & Inspiring Growth:** Daniels developed leadership programs within the department, mentoring future leaders and providing officers with career growth opportunities. This not only boosted morale but also built a stronger, more resilient team.

Results:

Within two years, the department saw increased officer engagement, improved community relations, and enhanced internal collaboration. By applying HEART principles, Chief Daniels transformed the department from a reactive force to a proactive, community-focused organization.

Key Takeaways

- 💜 *HEART* **Leadership is scalable:** Whether in law enforcement, corporate environments, or nonprofit organizations, applying emotional intelligence enhances organizational success.

- 💜 **Culture drives performance:** When leaders prioritize self-awareness, empathy, and growth, they create environments where people thrive and contribute at their highest level.

- 💜 **Sustainable leadership is intentional:** Embedding *HEART* principles into everyday operations ensures that leadership impact extends beyond individuals to the entire organization.

Final Reflection

Consider your leadership impact at an organizational level:

- 💜 Are you fostering self-awareness and emotional intelligence among leaders?

- 💜 How is empathy integrated into decision-making and team dynamics?

- 💜 Does your organization reinforce its purpose and provide growth opportunities for employees?

By applying *HEART* Leadership, you're creating a legacy of positive transformation that benefits both people and performance.

"Trust is the currency of leadership invest in emotional intelligence, and you will always lead with abundance."

~Your Therapy Doctor

Chapter 10:
Becoming a HEART Centered Leader:

Your Next Steps

Leadership is not a destination; it is a continuous journey of growth, self-awareness, and transformation. Becoming a *HEART*-centered leader means integrating emotional intelligence, resilience, and purpose into every decision and interaction. As you move forward, applying the *HEART Framework*, the *C.A.R.E.* Approach, and Leadership

Anchors will help you lead with intention, authenticity, and impact.

Practical Steps to Lean into HEART Leadership

Harness Self-Awareness

- ♥ Set aside time for self-reflection and journaling on your leadership experiences.
- ♥ Seek feedback from colleagues, mentors, and teams to identify blind spots.
- ♥ Take the EQ-i 2.0/360 Feedback Assessment to gain deep insights into your emotional intelligence strengths and areas for growth.

- ♥ Practice mindfulness and emotional regulation techniques to stay grounded.

Elevate Emotional Agility

- ♥ Develop coping strategies for high-pressure situations.
- ♥ Adapt to change with a growth mindset, viewing challenges as opportunities.
- ♥ Encourage a culture of resilience within your team by modeling composure and optimism.

Activate Empathy & Connection

- ♥ Strengthen your active listening skills by fully engaging in conversations.
- ♥ Foster inclusiveness by creating safe spaces for dialogue and collaboration.
- ♥ Regularly express appreciation and recognize the contributions of others.
- ♥ Use EQ-i 2.0 Group and Leadership Profiles to assess team dynamics and improve communication.

Reinforce Purpose & Vision

- ♥ Align your leadership with your core values and organizational mission.
- ♥ Clearly communicate vision and purpose to inspire and unify your team.
- ♥ Encourage team members to connect their personal goals with the bigger picture.

Transform & Inspire Growth

- ♥ Mentor and support emerging leaders by sharing knowledge and experiences.
- ♥ Invest in continuous learning through books, courses, and professional development.
- ♥ Challenge yourself and others to innovate and embrace new leadership perspectives.
- ♥ Utilize EQ assessments to track growth and adjust leadership strategies accordingly.

Applying the C.A.R.E. Approach to Daily Leadership

The *C.A.R.E.* Approach helps leaders create a psychologically safe, engaging, and growth-oriented work environment. As you apply it in your leadership practice, keep these actionable steps in mind:

- 💜 **Context:** Begin every conversation by framing the discussion with clarity and shared goals.
- 💜 **Affirmation:** Recognize strengths and contributions before addressing challenges.
- 💜 **Reflection:** Invite input and collaboration to promote accountability and engagement.
- 💜 **Encouragement:** Offer support, resources, and motivation to drive positive change.

By leading with *C.A.R.E.,* you ensure that every interaction fosters trust and confidence.

Anchoring Leadership for Long-Term Impact

Transformational leadership is rooted in three essential anchors: Process, Relationships, and Inspiration. To sustain your leadership impact:

- 💜 **Establish Strong Processes:** Create clear systems that support efficiency, accountability, and innovation.
- 💜 **Prioritize Meaningful Relationships:** Build trust through transparency, authenticity, and empathy.
- 💜 **Lead with Inspiration:** Communicate a compelling vision and empower others to take ownership of their success.

When these three anchors are consistently reinforced, they create a foundation for resilient, high-performing teams and organizations.

Conclusion: Leading with HEART in Every Interaction

The journey of leadership is never-ending, however, the choice to lead with *HEART* is one you make daily. By committing to self-awareness, emotional agility, empathy, purpose, and growth, you can cultivate an environment where people thrive, innovate, and feel valued. As you step forward, reflect on these guided questions:

- How will I integrate *HEART* principles into my leadership approach today?
- Where have I seen growth in my leadership so far?
- What actions can I take to create a culture of trust, engagement, and empowerment?
- What habits or mindsets do I need to strengthen?
- How will I continue to develop myself and others in this ongoing leadership journey?
- How will I stay committed to emotional intelligence in my everyday leadership?

Leadership is about being open, adaptable, and intentional in how you show up for those around you. Keep leading with *HEART*, and you will not only transform your leadership, you will also leave a lasting, positive impact on those you serve.

"The most powerful leader is the one who leads with both wisdom and heart, balancing strategy with empathy."

~Your Therapy Doctor 🖤

Take the
Workplace Resilience
Quiz

Take Resilient Leadership Quiz using the QR Code above. Start your journey to Emotional Intelligence.

A Personal Letter from Your Therapy Doctor

Dear Leader,

I want to take a moment to acknowledge you, your commitment, your growth and your willingness to step into a deeper level of leadership. The fact that you've made it to this point in the book tells me that you are serious about transformation, not just for yourself, but for those you lead that is powerful.

Here's what I know: **leadership isn't about perfection. It's about progress.**

There will be moments when you don't have all the answers. Days when challenges test your patience and dare I say tolerance. Times when emotions run high. The difference between good leaders and great ones is simple; great leaders choose to respond with intention, not impulse.

So, I ask you:

- 💜 How will you use emotional intelligence to lead with clarity and authenticity?

100

- ♥ How will you build a culture of trust, resilience, and empowerment?
- ♥ How will you keep showing up, even when leadership feels heavy?

You already have everything you need within you. This book has given you the tools however the real magic happens when you use them consistently.

As you move forward, I encourage you to embrace these three commitments:

- ♥ **Commit to Self-Awareness** – Keep learning about yourself, your triggers and how you impact others.
- ♥ **Commit to Compassionate Leadership** – Lead with empathy, even in difficult conversations.
- ♥ **Commit to Growth** – Stay open to learning, adapting and refining your leadership approach.

Leadership is a calling. The fact that you're here means you're ready to lead in a way that is impactful, transformative, and deeply intentional. I believe in you. Keep going. You got this!

With Heart,

Dr Pauline Belton, Your Therapy Doctor ♥

Visit http://www.yourtherapydoctor.com
to learn more or use the QR code
below to start your journey.

Notes

_____

_____

_____

_____

_____

_____

_____

_____

_____

_____

_____

_____

_____

_____

_____

Next Steps

_____

_____

_____

Notes

_____

_____

_____

_____

_____

_____

_____

_____

_____

_____

_____

_____

_____

_____

Next Steps

_____

_____

_____

Notes

_____

_____

_____

_____

_____

_____

_____

_____

_____

_____

_____

_____

_____

_____

_____

Next Steps

_____

_____

_____

Notes

_____
_____
_____
_____
_____
_____
_____
_____
_____
_____
_____
_____
_____
_____

Next Steps

_____
_____
_____

The HEART Framework

*The **HEART** Framework*
A practical model for resilient,
emotionally intelligent leadership

Harness - Self Awareness
Understand yourself before leading
other

Elevated - Emotional Agility
Learn to regulate emotions and
respond to challenges with clarity

Activate - Empathy & Connection
Foster strong relationships and trust

Reinforcement - Purpose & Vision
Align leadership with your core values
and inspire your team

Transform - Inspire Growth
Develop future leaders and create a
lasting impact

The C.A.R.E. Framework

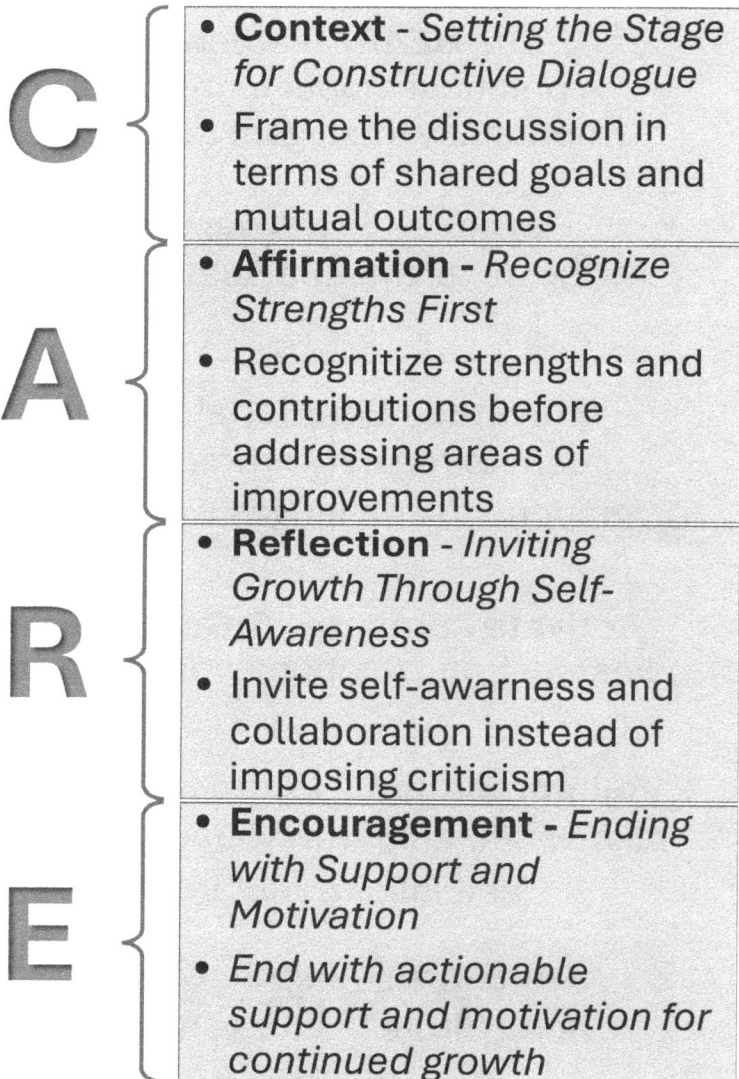

C {

- **Context** - *Setting the Stage for Constructive Dialogue*
- Frame the discussion in terms of shared goals and mutual outcomes

A {

- **Affirmation** - *Recognize Strengths First*
- Recognitize strengths and contributions before addressing areas of improvements

R {

- **Reflection** - *Inviting Growth Through Self-Awareness*
- Invite self-awarness and collaboration instead of imposing criticism

E {

- **Encouragement** - *Ending with Support and Motivation*
- *End with actionable support and motivation for continued growth*

www.ingramcontent.com/pod-product-compliance
Lightning Source LLC
Chambersburg PA
CBHW071434210326
41597CB00020B/3791